The Everlasting Friendship

Stork Birds and Humans

African Fable

Written, and illustrated by: Billy Moro-Wey

African Games

The Everlasting Friendship

Stork Birds and Humans
African Fable

Written, and Illustrated by:

Billy Moro-Wey

Copyright © 2024 Billy Moro-Wey

ISBN (Hardback): 979-8-89381-069-1
ISBN (Paperback): 979-8-89381-070-7
ISBN (eBook): 979-8-89381-071-4

All rights reserved. No part of this book may
be reproduced or transmitted in any form or by any means, electronic or
mechanical, including photocopying, recording, or by any information storage and retrieval
system, without permission in writing from the copyright owner.

The views expressed in this work are solely those
of the author and do not necessarily reflect the views of the publisher, and the
publisher hereby disclaims any responsibility for them.

508 West 26th Street KEARNEY, NE 68848
402-819-3224
info@medialiteraryexcellence.com

Contents

Chapter 1 1
Chapter 2 9
Chapter 3 18
Chapter 4 25
Chapter 5 32
Chapter 6 39
Chapter 7 45
Chapter 8 52
Chapter 9 61
Chapter 10 64
Chapter 11 67
Chapter 12 82

This book is dedicated to my,
Beloved parents and Dorota

Chapter 1

FAR AWAY IN AFRICA, in a village called Odi along the banks of River Nun; humans and stork birds developed an everlasting friendship, that has been known from generation to generations.

Odi Village

The Kilolo family was the first in the village to have a stork's nest built on the roof of the family house.

Stork bird nest on house roof

Okiniki, the head of the family, had a wife called Ebibo and they had two beloved children, a boy and a girl named Ndoki and Nyoyo respectively.

The Kilolo Family

How did the Kilolo family become the first to have a stork's nest built on the roof of the family house?

Early on a Saturday morning, Okiniki went to the forest to carve a canoe from a very big trunk of an Iroko tree, which he felled some days back,

The canoe carving

and possibly hunt for some wild animals, or do fishing on his way back home.

Meanwhile, his wife decided to go alone to their farm a couple of miles into the bush, to harvest some yam, coco yam and tapioca for food over the weekend and pick up some bush mangoes for the children to enjoy.

> Generally, in this village, men provided meat and fish for cooking meals, while women grew farm produce to feed the family with.

Ebibo, gave the children breakfast. Then, she picked up a basket and proceeded on her way to the farm.

Ebibo's trip to the farm begins

They waved her good-bye and she waved back at them. Then, she vanished into the bush a few minutes later while the children looked on, daydreaming.

The children looking at their mother

The children wondered when their mother would allow them accompany her to the farm. That may be a dream come true for them at their current age.

Chapter 2

EBIBO WALKED FOR ABOUT a mile into the bush and saw a lonely snake gliding towards her along the pathway.

Ebibo's encounter with the snake

So, she decided to stop, and ask the snake what it was doing around alone.
"Snake, are you alright, and what are you doing here all by yourself?" she enquired.

Ebibo and the snake's interrogation

"Oh! Thanks to God, you are here to save me from this terrible cold I am feeling now; I am almost freezing to death and I need a warm shelter for a short while," the snake quipped.

"Where can you get such a warm shelter in this bush? Ebibo gestured.

The snake said, "I guess you can help me."

"But how?" Ebibo asked.

Ebibo asks "how?"

"Please allow me enter and stay in your belly for a short while, to enable me warm up, and I promise to crawl out as soon as I feel warm enough and better."

Ebibo, being a very kind woman, considered the snake's request and asked.

"Do you really promise to come out immediately afterwards?"

"I promise."

Ebibo then bent down, and picked up the snake.

Ebibo picks up the snake

She took the snake into her mouth, and allowed it glide into her stomach.

Ebibo took the snake into her mouth

> Snake got into Ebibo's stomach and found that it was more like being in a paradise. It was compact, moist, warm and very comfortable. The snake then decided to make it his new home

Ebibo felt the need for her to reach the farm on time to do her harvesting. But the thought of having the snake in her stomach made her to feel rather uncomfortable standing in the middle of the forest, not proceeding to the farm.

After a short while, Ebibo deliberated on the fact that the snake had had enough time to warm up inside her, and felt it was time for it to vacate her stomach. In order to remove strain from her legs, Ebibo sat down on the ground before calling out to the snake again.

Ebibo sat down and waited

"Hey snake, how are you feeling? Isn't it time for you to come out, please?"

"I feel like I am in heaven here. It is really very comfortable."

"Snake, you may feel comfortable inside me but I'm not, and besides, I need to proceed to the farm and gather food-stuff for my family," Ebibo warned.

"Well, I'm sorry woman but I don't want to leave this wonderful shelter, I will rather remain inside your stomach, if you don't mind."

"What do you mean by, if I don't mind, snake, are you really serious?"

"Honestly, I can't be more serious." Ebibo became very worried and said, "but you promised to come out as soon as you feel better, isn't it?"
"Yes, but I have changed my mind."

Ebibo felt the need for an immediate help from someone to persuade the snake to crawl out of her stomach.

Chapter 3

EBIBO LOOKED AROUND and saw a young, elegant palm tree just a few yards away from her. She walked over to the palm tree, and related her horrible experience with the snake to it.

She mentioned the fact that she had been kind enough to allow the snake to crawl into her stomach to warm up itself for a short while and come out afterwards; so that she could proceed on her trip to the farm. But the snake has refused to vacate her stomach, thereby disregarding their previous agreement.

"Please palm tree, can you help me persuade the snake to come out of my stomach?"

Ebibo pleads to the palm tree

"No, I am sorry but I cannot do that, because you humans are not good to my kind. You inflict pain on us in various ways, for example:

1. By drilling and cutting holes into our trunks, forcing us to reluctantly bleed away our precious juice, which you use for palm wine.

Keg of Palm Wine

2. You mercilessly cut our branches and fronds for sweeping your floors and thatching the roof of your houses. You also spread our kernel on the ground around your houses to stop erosion, and create murals on your walls with our kernel.

3. You ungratefully use our flesh and fibrous roots for your foot mats.

Foot Mat

4. You lay our trunks across streams and wide gutters in form of unpaid for bridges.

Palm Trunk Bridge

5. You carelessly undermine our fruit, but you cannot do without the oil it provides for your cooking.

Bunch of Palm Fruit

Bottle of Palm Oil

Yet at no time did human beings thank us. If you would be sincere to yourself, do see any reason why I should like to help you?"

> Ebibo was aghast and knew that the palm tree's woes were just but true, because some human beings don't respect most of other living things.

At that moment, the snake was very glad that the palm tree refused to help the woman.

Chapter 4

ON THE SAME MORNING, a donkey decided to go into the forest and see what life really looks like for wild animals. It had talks with several types of animals.

He discovered that life in the forest is based on survival of the fittest. If you are smart and lucky, you can live long.

But there is an imminent danger of being captured by humans. The good thing about being in the forest is that nobody forces you to do those things you may not want to do at a particular time.

The donkey was on its way back to the village when he met and saw Ebibo looking morose and sad.

The donkey called out to her.
"Hey woman, what are you doing here alone and looking so sad?"

Ebibo's encounter with the donkey

Ebibo gestured and said, "I was on my way to the farm when I met and agreed to help snake, who was feeling terribly cold and shivering. Snake said he needed a shelter for a short time in order to warm up, and promised to crawl out afterwards if I should allow it to take shelter in my stomach. So, I decided to help, and allowed it to crawl through my mouth into my stomach. But unfortunately, snake did not keep its promise, instead, it has decided to stay permanently in my stomach, because it is comfortable there."

    The donkey listened attentively to the woman's story, and asked the snake if that was true? The snake confirmed her story and said, "I intend to remain here for as long as it is possible."

"Snake, it seems like you are being ungrateful, by not keeping your promise; but I would not persuade you to come out of the woman's stomach because:

> Some human beings are cruel to my kind.

1. They packed us up with very heavy loads and forced us to go on long trips.

Heavily loaded donkey

2. They kicked us on the sides and forced us to move faster, even when we were tired and needed some rest.

Donkey kicked on the side

3. They called us stupid, because of our gentleness, and expected us to perform our duties well.

Sorry woman, but I don't feel obligated to help you out of your present predicament."

> Ebibo was totally flabbergasted and disappointed with the donkey's opinionated decision and felt hopeless while the snake sang its song of victory.

Chapter 5

EBIBO MOVED TOWARD the farm and walked up to a banana tree with almost ripe banana fruit.

Ebibo and the banana tree

"Hi banana tree, please bear me out of this problem I have with a snake inside my stomach."

"What is a snake doing inside you," the banana tree asked?

Ebibo expressed how she showed kindness to the snake by allowing it to warm up inside her stomach for a short while only to regret it immediately, because snake had refused to fulfill its promise of coming out of her stomach afterwards."

The banana tree said. "That's exactly what you humans do to us, being ungrateful always."

1. "You indiscriminately eat our fruit raw, or fried when they are ripe. You boil them for food when they are unripe."

"Have you ever thanked us for providing you with the fruit?"

Eating banana

2. "You use our leaves to package your special diets."

Packaging

3. "You also seal your cooking pot with our leaves for great flavor."

Sealed cooking pot

4. "You cut our trunks for your children to play with, humiliate us, and throw to the garbage afterwards."

"Have you ever found it necessary to say sorry to us each time you cut us into pieces?"

Children playing with banana trunks

5. "It is a common thing that you humans at times beautify your yards with our trees, and use us for fencing as well."

Decorating and fencing

6. "When it rains, our leaves serve as umbrellas for you humans."

Banana leaf umbrella

"Do you really want to hear more woes from me, woman? Just like I said before, you humans don't know how to say thank you for all we've been doing for you. Rather, you keep on exploiting us with indiscriminate disrespect.

Therefore, I don't feel obliged to help you out of your current problem with the snake."

The snake rejoiced inside the woman's stomach and decided to stay intact for as long as possible. While Ebibo left the banana tree and proceeded towards the farm dejected.

Chapter 6

EBIBO'S FEAR THAT THE SNAKE might make her stomach its home escalated, and she became desperate to find relief from anyone who can save her from this terrible difficulty. However, she was still determined to reach the farm and harvest the food stuff necessary for the weekend.

> Monkeys normally feel that they are most related to humans because of the close facial resemblance. Therefore, in most cases, they seek human company. But unfortunately, they soon realized that humans don't share the same thoughts like them.

So, on this fateful day, Ebibo in her most sorrowful moment saw a monkey perched between two branches of a tree; and thought that this might be a ray of hope for her.

Ebibo and the monkey

The monkey teased Ebibo and asked her what she was doing out there alone in the bush. But on a closer look, it saw that something was wrong with her, because she seemed to be very unhappy. "Hey woman! You look worried, are you alright?"

"No! I am not alright with a snake in my stomach, most especially when it has refused to come out. Please could you help convince snake to vacate my stomach like it promised to do before entering me?"

"Uh….!"

The monkey exclaimed and thought for a moment before responding to Ebibo's plea.

"Why should I help you, after the ordeals you humans put me and my kind through to satisfy your egos?"

    1. "You place us in zoos for people to observe and laugh at, because we are funny, playful and jolly."

At the zoo

2. "At times, you make us participate in circuses against our will."

Monkey and a bear in circus

3. "You hunt us down and sell our meat for food."
4. "You disrespect simple facts that monkeys and humans have similar facial structure."

Monkey's close resemblance to human facial structure

'I am indeed very sorry woman, I would have loved to help you, but I cannot do so under these circumstances.

Ebibo was surprised that humans don't have many friends among other living things, but she was still determined to reach the farm.

Chapter 7

BEES ARE FOUND in every type of vegetation in Africa.

A bee

They live either inside the hole of a tree trunk, in the crevices of rock or containers with hollow space; where they build honeycombs for storing the honey they produce.

Honeycomb and honey

But when they are in transit looking out for a new home, they stay together in a bunch hanging from the branch of a tree.

On this fateful day, a band of bees was on its way to a new location after some humans had set fire on their previous home and removed their honeycombs and honey. During this process, a lot of bees got burnt to death while the remaining ones helplessly escaped together to a different location.

Honey hunting with fire by humans

The bunch of bees loomed from the branch of a tree, and the soldier bees watched out for intruders when Ebibo showed up.

Ebibo and the bunch of bees

Ebibo conferred within herself to seek help from the bees, because she was feeling terribly concerned that she might not be able to get rid of the snake from her stomach.

"Good morning bees," Ebibo saluted.

"Good morning woman," the bees said in unison. Ebibo walked closer to the bunch of bees, and fervently requested their help to persuade snake to crawl out of her stomach as previously agreed upon.

She related the story of how the snake seriously needed help; which she rendered in good faith. But she was terribly disappointed with the snake's ingratitude later, because snake has bluntly refused to crawl out of her stomach after being warmed up like it promised to do.

The leader of the bees called out to the snake to know if what the woman said was true. The snake said "yes, pretty much so."

"But why did you decide to remain in her stomach?" the bee asked.

'It is like heaven in here, and I don't want to lose such an opportunity, the snake murmured. "And besides, you probably would have done the same thing like me if you had the chance" The bee thought for a while and said, "I don't blame you for what you are doing now, because some humans don't have sympathy nor respect for other living things. Human beings like you have just burnt down our home and removed our valuable honeycomb and honey. That is why we are here hanging from the branch of this tree like homeless nonentities."

"Woman, I am sorry but we cannot assist you with your problem," the bee declared.

The snake danced inside Ebibo's stomach, and caused her much pain. The bees decided that they had rested enough and it was time for them to continue their journey in search of a new home. They all flew away from the presence of the woman.

Ebibo felt highly dejected but summed up courage to convince the snake to please vacate her stomach and possibly be a man of its words. The snake said, "no and never ever again." But Ebibo still continued her trip to the farm.

Chapter 8

THE TROPICAL TEMPERATURE was gaining momentum and its effect was telling much on the vegetation and its inhabitants.

> While Ebibo contemplated on how to get rid of the snake inside her stomach; a group of stork birds took advantage of the good weather and decided to show their young ones the beauty of the vegetation.

The young stork birds were old enough to fly a couple of miles but not too far, because their wings were still weak for long distance flights. Besides, at this time of the day, it was just natural that the parents should lead the young ones to a place where they could fetch something to eat. So, the group of stork birds chattered and flew low over the vegetation where Ebibo was making her way to the farm.

Ebibo and the stork birds flying over

Ebibo heard birds chattering above her and therefore she looked up into the sky. She saw a group of happy stork birds and decided to call out and beckon to them at that very moment they were flying directly above her.

'Hey, hey, stork birds, please come over here. I seriously need your help."

The stork birds looked down at Ebibo; and the leader of the group commanded them to land and see what was so important and wrong with the woman below.

No sooner the group landed in front of Ebibo, the birds observed that she was very unhappy, and almost at the verge of crying.

The leader of the stork birds asked the woman; "why do you look so unhappy?"

Stork leader talking to Ebibo

Ebibo said, "thank you for coming by. I really need your help because I have a snake inside my stomach right now; and it has refused to come out in contradiction to our previous agreement." "That is very strange, but how did the snake manage to get into your stomach in the first place? Were you sleeping when it crawled inside you or how else did it happen?" The stork birds were perplexed.

> The woman had to retell the story of what happened to her on the way to the farm, since she left home that morning.

"I was on my way to the farm to harvest some food stuff to feed my family with over the weekend, when I met this lonely snake barely crawling and shivering along the pathway to the farm. I then asked the snake what it was doing out there alone.

The snake said that it was freezing and needed a shelter for a short while to warm up and later go back to its kind.

"Where can you find such a shelter in the middle of the forest?" I asked.

Then the snake suggested that I should please allow it crawl into my stomach to warm up for a short while, and promised to vacate my stomach immediately it felt a little better.

I decided to do the snake that favor, only to regret it immediately afterwards, because the snake failed to keep its promise.

Rather, the snake said that my stomach is very comfortable and it's more like a paradise. Therefore, it sees no reason why it should not remain in my stomach forever."

Ebibo relays her story to the stork birds

"Oh, oh!" all the stork birds exclaimed in unison. The leader of the stork birds pitied and sympathized with the woman, and said; "woman, please wait a moment and allow me consult with my family first."

The stork birds rallied together, some yards away from the woman, so that the snake might not hear their plan on how to lure the snake out of the woman's stomach.

Stork birds consulting together

They decided that the snake must be convinced to show its face through the woman's mouth while talking to them; and then the leader will strike unexpectedly to pull the snake out of the woman's mouth.

So, the leader of the stork birds returned to the woman, while its comrades and children stood by ready to render any help, if it became necessary.

Chapter 9

WHEN THE LEADER OF THE STORK BIRDS came back to the woman, she wasn't sure whether she would receive the help she direly needed from them. At the same time inside her stomach, the snake also wondered whether or not the stork birds have decided to find a way to get rid of it from the woman's stomach.

> *The leader of the stork birds thought of the fact that humans have generally been good to their kind, and therefore, there is no reason why they should not help this woman with the ungrateful snake inside her stomach. Therefore, the leader wanted a confirmation of the woman's story from the snake.*

"Woman, I have heard your own side of the story, but how am I sure that the snake does not have something contrary to yours?" The leader of the stork birds quipped.

Ebibo said, "please ask the snake if I wasn't telling the truth."

"Then, snake, would you confirm the woman's story about what you did to her as being true?" The leader of the birds asked.

"Pretty much so." The snake answered from inside the woman's stomach. "You don't have an idea of how comfortable it is in here, and I might just love to make this wonderful shelter my home for the rest of my life."

"Snake, I thought you promised the woman that you will crawl out of her stomach after warming up for a short while. What then makes you a man of your own words, if you break the promise? The leader of the birds teased.

"Sometimes people break laws, so also a promise can be broken. Please leave me alone." The snake exclaimed.

"If you want me to leave you alone, then you will have to talk to me face to face, man to man first before I make my decisions, and please stop talking to me from inside the woman's stomach," the leader of the birds requested.

"No, I don't want to talk to you." The snake screamed.

Chapter 10

THE LEADER OF THE STORK BIRDS *saw that the snake was adamant and can be convinced to vacate the woman's stomach only through strict diplomacy.*

> The stork bird gave the woman a sign not worry about the turn of events. Then it suddenly talked to the snake in a friendly manner.

"Hey snake, please don't get me wrong. I am not here to condemn you, knowing fully well that opportunities like you have right now come once in a lifetime. I will not force you to think otherwise if you don't want to. But please be a gentleman, at least to show your face and say hello to my children and comrades. My young children are very anxious to see a snake's beautiful face for the first time in their life, after hearing so many good things about you and your race."

"Why should I trust you stork?" the snake asked inquisitively.

"Well, seeing is what you believe in snake, won't you like to see the people who are greeting you at least?" the stork asked in a friendly manner.

"Yes of course, but supposing that's a trap?" "No, it is not a trap, rather my children will be very appreciative of your kindness. Please, all you need do is just show your face through the woman's mouth, say hello to my people and you can return to your wonderful shelter."

"Is that a promise stork?"

"Yes of course snake."

"Then tell the woman to open her mouth slightly for me to peep and greet your children and comrades. Thereafter, I will return to my comfortable shelter," the snake demanded.

"Great, snake, that's pretty kind of you. I always knew that you are a gentleman. Let me just instruct the woman to open up her mouth as you demanded," the leader of the stork bird said with happiness.

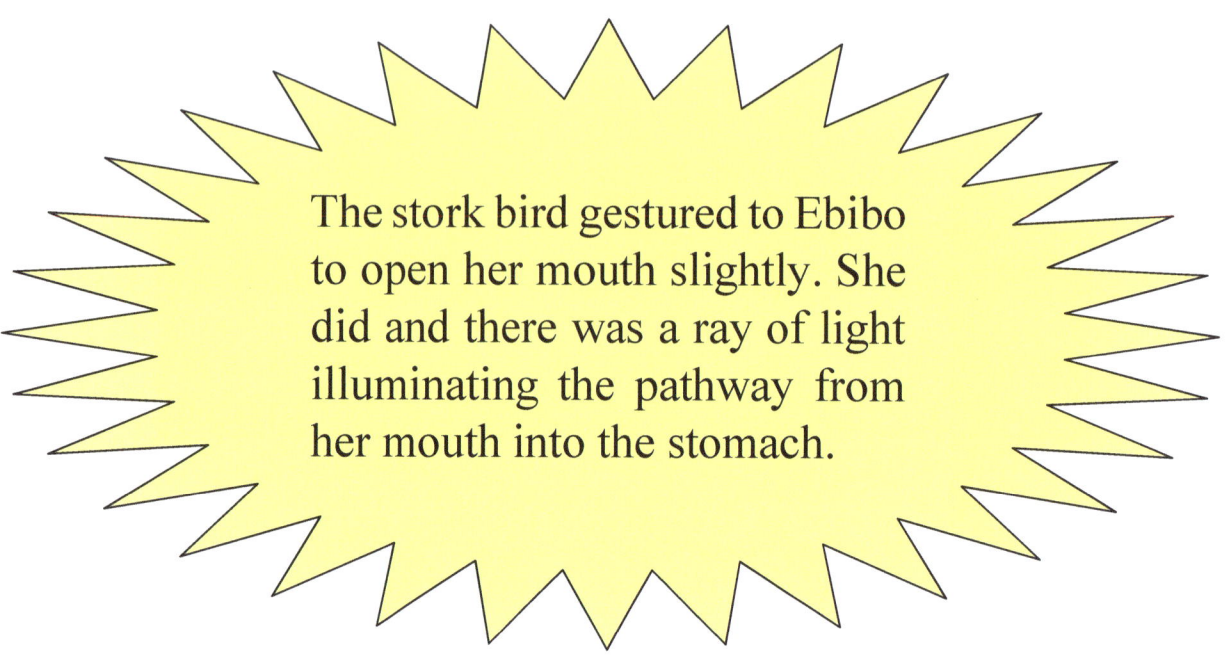

The stork bird gestured to Ebibo to open her mouth slightly. She did and there was a ray of light illuminating the pathway from her mouth into the stomach.

The snake saw the light and called out to the leader of the stork birds to inform that it was on its way out to peep and greet his children and comrades.

At that very moment, the leader of the stork birds gestured to its people to come closer to meet the snake.

Chapter 11

THE SNAKE CRAWLED FROM Ebibo's stomach and carefully approached her slightly opened mouth, peeped, and then announced, "I am here stork."

Snake shows up

"Oh snake, isn't that great of you to show up?" the leader of the stork birds complimented.

Stork compliments snake

"Now that you are visible, my children and comrades can admire your beauty snake, don't you think so?"
"Well, beauty is in the eye of the beholder stork", the snake countered.

Stork shows snake to its children and comrades

At that moment the children of the stork bird become very anxious to take a good look at a snake for the first time in their lives. So, they moved a little closer, and one of them said, "Wow! The snake looks slick and cute. It is a pity we cannot see beyond its head. I wish it could show us a little more of itself."

Another child complimented the snake's adorable green eyes and said, "I wish I had similar eyes like the snake's."

Meanwhile, the snake felt so proud of itself after listening to so many praises from the stork's children, and forgot the need to be extra careful. It smiled to show its extremely white teeth and felt great satisfaction when the stork's children and comrades smiled back at it.

The leader of the stork birds gestured and asked its people to salute the snake. They all said "hello snake" in unison and in a very friendly manner. Then they took off, as previously planned when they had the last consultation.

The snake felt at ease with its new friends and got carried away by their friendliness. But what it could not understand was why they took off all of a sudden.

The snake asked. "Why are they leaving so suddenly?"

The leader of the stork birds explained to the snake that its people like talking to friends one on one, and not when part of your body is hidden. So please show up at least a little more of your cute body for them to see.

Snake about saying hello to storks

That will encourage them to come back and exchange greetings with you.

"Can I trust you, stork?"

"Absolutely"

"Ok, I will show a little more of my body." Then the leader of the storks thanked the snake heartily and called the flock back to land.

The snake could not resist the temptation and therefore crawled forward in the woman's mouth to show a little more of its body, faced the storks and unsuspectingly said "hi" to them with a big smile.

The wonderful and long- awaited moment finally arrived. So, the leader of the stork birds jumped up and at the speed of lightening struck the snake's head with its, solid beak, and pulled the snake out of the woman's mouth with a single upward stroke.

Stork pulling snake out with a stroke

The stork bird smashed the snake on the ground in front of the woman and everybody else, and placed a strong foot on the snake's head to pin it down.

Stork pinned down the snake's head

The snake wriggled and screamed vehemently with its head pinned down, and shamelessly begged for mercy.

> Everybody around screamed with joy and excitement to see the snake, now on the begging side.

The snake suddenly tried to prove tough and said, "but stork, that was a breach of trust. You promised to let me go back into the woman's stomach after I must have met your people; you are not trustworthy.

"Oh, yes? Wasn't that exactly what you did to the woman earlier today? My friend snake, please always remember that what goes around comes around."

Everybody around said in unison, "that's right." "What shall we do to the snake, kill it or we let it go?" The stork birds asked in unison.

> The woman inferred that, "an eye for an eye does not show wisdom, and therefore suggested; how about if we let it go, on the grounds that the snake promises never to do such bad things to people again?"

"Yes! I will be good to people generally from now on, after on I have learned my lesson," the snake promised.

Unanimously they agreed to release the snake. So, the leader of the stork bird asked the woman for a last wish. She had no wishes therefore it lifted its foot from the snake's head, granting it freedom to glide away into the forest.

> The children of the stork bird watched with fascination as the disgraced snake glided into the surrounding bush, but wondered how much of an ingrate the snake had been to the woman .

The snake glides away in disgrace

Ebibo beamed and danced with happiness, because she finally got rid of the snake with the help of the stork birds. Then she openly invited the birds.

Ebibo danced with the storks

"You are welcome to stop by at our village anytime you want. My family house is the first one from the south as you enter the village, and it is very close to the tallest coconut tree." She shook hands with the birds and continued with her speech.

Ebibo shaking hands with the birds

"Your action today has proved beyond reasonable doubt that you are true friends; because a friend in need is a friend indeed."

An undeniable friendship between humans and stork birds was born from that day on till date.

The stork birds were very appreciative for the woman's invitation and promised to honor it someday in the near future.

Then Ebibo and the stork birds exchanged their departing greetings; and the birds took off into the sky to continue their adventure, while Ebibo picked up her basket and resumed her trip to the farm to harvest some foodstuff for her family to enjoy over the weekend.

The stork birds took off into the sky

Chapter 12

Ebibo walked briskly and hummed a tune as she marched toward the farm, because she was now in a better mood after finally getting rid of the snake from her stomach.

Ebibo picking bush mango

On the way to the farm, Ebibo picked some bush mangoes from the ground into her basket for her children to enjoy at home.

At the farm, Ebibo dug out some yam and tapioca tubers, which she placed inside the basket along with the mangoes.

Ebibo digging tubers

Then, she placed the full basket on her head and proceeded back home, with the amazing story of her encounter with the snake to relay to her family.

> Ebibo's children have been really worried about why their mother had stayed so long in the farm. She was supposed to have returned home long time ago. Their father had also not returned home from the forest, where he went to carve a canoe. But the children were already used to his long absences. So, the two sat in front of their house waiting for their parents' arrival back home.

Ebibo was about a hundred yards away from home when the children saw her and ran out to meet her before she reached home.

The children running to meet Ebibo

Ebibo's love flowed towards her children, and she was extremely happy to see them after the terrible ordeal she had with the snake. *She equally smiled at the fact that a new friendship between storks and humans was born, during the occasion when the storks saved her from the ungrateful hands of the snake.*

www.ingramcontent.com/pod-product-compliance
Lightning Source LLC
Chambersburg PA
CBHW061155030426
42337CB00002B/18